Feedback on "Tending the Light"

"Mary Beth Magee's poetry collection is a heartfelt exploration of faith, community, and endurance. Through gentle yet evocative language, Magee conveys the importance of staying grounded in one's convictions, even in turbulent times. Her use of imagery, particularly in poems like "Tending the Light" and "Endurance," effectively illustrates the steadfast presence of God's love amidst life's challenges."

Diane Williams
Author, Storyteller
Retired Art Administrator
https://amzn.to/3QTElt9

"Well done! I enjoyed it."

Laura Anne Ewald
Author, Puppeteer, Speaker
The Power of Story
https://www.lauraanneewald.com/

Tending the Light

Mary Beth Magee

Mississippi Poetry Society

2025 Poet of the Year

BOTR Press

Poplarville, Mississippi

Copyright 2025   Mary Beth Magee
Published by BOTR Press

Cover art by Courtney Corlew
Section page art by firkin
Graphics by Mary Beth Magee

This is a work of original poetry. No AI was used in the writing of these poems. All verses are the original work of Mary Beth Magee except where quotations are used and identified.

ISBN: 978-1-7378103-5-3

Table of Contents

Tending the Light of Writing

Tending the Light

Mary Beth Magee

Dedication

This collection is dedicated to my son and his family, the most precious jewels of my life. I love you with all my heart.

To the parents, grandparents, sisters, brothers, aunts, uncles, cousins, whether blood born or adopted over the years, thank you for your love and all the crazy experiences which help fuel my poetry.

To Trudy, the "Patron of the Arts" who keeps me going.

To my dear friends in the Mississippi Poetry Society. You have encouraged me, challenged me and led me to become better than I thought I could be. You are treasures of my heart for all time.

To the memory of my MPS friend, Judy Davies. She always encouraged me to "Go for it!" I miss her so much.

Thanks to those who helped with proofing and editing these works. Laura Anne Ewald, the amazing author of "The Power of Story" and founder of The Everyman

Puppet Theatre. I am blessed to have your friendship.

Finally – and most importantly – to my Lord and Savior Jesus Christ, the Light in my lighthouse, the anchor of my life.

Introduction

I am a woman of odd combinations. I was born in the city, but prefer a rural lifestyle. Dog lover my whole life. I love cats, but allergic to them. Love to read, love to write.

Mother of one, grandmother to one. I've been married, divorced then tried again and that one failed, too. I believe in the institution of marriage but no longer seek it for myself.

My "extended" family includes wonderful people of a wide assortment of ages, backgrounds and ethnicities. They graciously let me love them and be a part of their respective worlds. How rich I am!

I've lived longer, grown far older than I ever thought I would. How did that happen?

As a writer, I am a poet as well as a journalist. I write fiction, nonfiction, children's books and devotions. Being named the Mississippi Poetry Society 2025 Poet of the Year is an honor I treasure.

As a Christian who has been a part of several denominations over the years, I know in my heart God's cares less about my label than my soul. I love the Lord and always seek to do His will, although – being human – I sometimes fail. I'm so grateful He loves me anyway.

This collection of poems seeks to honor my Creator and the Son He sent to buy my pardon. I thank Him for the many gifts He has given and praise Him for His wondrous works. To God be the glory!

I hope these verses will remind you of how precious He is – the Light of the World, and they will bless you on your journey.

Mary Beth Magee

April 2025

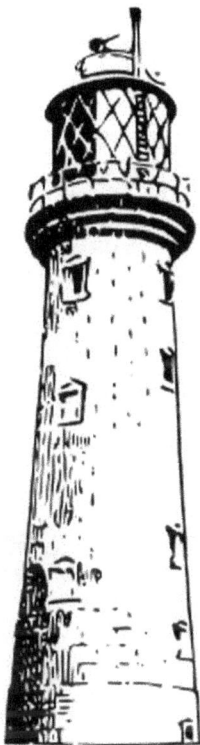

Tending the Light of Faith

To grow in faith requires a commitment, a dedication. Our light can only shine as brightly as the fuel we feed it permits. May these verses feed *your* light.

Tending the Light

Before electronics and satellites
Sailors looked to the coast for guiding lights.
There on the shore stood a building alone.
A keeper dwelled there to make sure light
    shone
Through the cruelest storm and the darkest
    night.
For mariners, it was a welcome sight.
How many lives have been saved through
    their care?
How many ships did the lighthouses spare?
The lonely light, lit and tended, cared for,
Guided the courses of ships and sailors.
Like lighthouses, we have been called to
    shine,
To share God's great love for His world so
    fine.
We stand in the storm of a lost, mad land
Shining the beacon of God's love for man.
To keep our lights bright, we must do our
    parts
To reflect God's love through our servant
    hearts.
We tend to our lights with study and prayer,
That we may learn more about how we can
    care

(continued)

For fellow beings who may be in need.
May our diligence serve to plant a seed
Which spreads as does the lighthouse's
    bright glow
That others our Father's love may then
    know.

A Passion

Do you have
A passion for Jesus?
Pass it on for Jesus.
Tell others of His love
And His sacrifice.
Share the word of eternal life
With those who haven't heard.
Take your passion for Jesus
And pass it on for Jesus,
For the sake of the world.

Endurance

"He brings eternal life, which gives light to everyone. His light shines brightly, cutting the darkness, and the darkness has no power to put it out."
(John 1:4-5, paraphrase)

Waves crash against the cliff face,
Sending spray high into the night air.
Hurricanes in the heat,
Blizzards in the cold,
Yet the lighthouse stands.
Blazing sun bakes its painted brick by day
Making its white stripes gleam against the
    landscape.
Moonlight reflects from its angled lens at
    night,
Rippling across the glass in its delicate
    dance.
Darkness threatens to devour it on
    moonless nights,
Yet the lighthouse stands.
The beam of its mighty beacon sweeps the
    sky,
Marking a channel, or warning of rocks,
Letting mariners know where they are.
Through the corridor of years,
The long days and dark nights,
The lighthouse endures.
Like God's love, it shines, it guides, it
    endures.

Expert Opinions

I hear the experts talking on TV,
They theorize the way that things must be,
Expounding on the birth of space and time.
Using words which jar and seldom rhyme.
Acronyms contrived to tell a story
Fly about in their initialed glory.
The more they talk, the more I find I know
That those expert opinions come and go.
What once we thought we knew with
    certainty
And counted on as bedrock fact, you see,
May not hold true with new discovery.
As they tout "truths" which "rewrite" history.
In my expert opinion, I can vow
We will know more tomorrow than right
    now.
And when we meet our Maker face to face
The Expert of all experts will erase
Our doubts and questions as He lets us see
The truth of how things work and came to
    be.

Dawning

Fingers of rose and gold fight clear
Of dark night's grasp so cold and drear.
Moment by moment, dawn creeps through,
Showing a day that's born brand new.
Rejoice, oh dawn, and celebrate
This precious day. I just can't wait
To see the treasures God will share
Within this dawning day so fair.

Unleash Your Light

*"Arise, shine; for thy light is come, and the glory of
the Lord is risen upon thee."*
(Isaiah 60:1, King James Version)

The light within you signals clear
You hold the blessed Savior dear.
So, shine your light for all to see
That they be called to turn the key
Which leads believers to the cross
To find redemption out of loss.
He gave His blood to let us shine,
To save our souls, both yours and mine.

The Steadfast Light

"Let your light so shine before men, that they may see your good works, and glorify your Father which is in heaven." (Matthew 5:16, King James Version)

Some lights shine openly for a time,
Bright and cheerful,
Then flicker and fail.
A gust of wind, a careless breath
Can extinguish them,
Leaving darkness all around.
Others glow within the embrace
Of a protective glass chimney,
Casting their subtle warmth
Steadily around the room.
Given sufficient fuel and a trimmed wick,
They will share their light forever,
With a gentle, helpful glow.
Brightest of all is the beam shining
Through the carefully aligned prisms of a
    lens
Set atop a lighthouse.
Strong, steadfast, dependable,
It lights the path of those at sea
Guiding them safely home.
Lord, let me be a steadfast lighthouse in
    Your service.
Let me shine my little light through the
    prism of Your love
That it can be magnified
To point weary hearts toward You.

Prayer in the Storm

*"And he arose, and rebuked the wind, and said unto
the sea, Peace, be still. And the wind ceased, and
there was a great calm."*
(Mark 4:39, King James Version)

In the teeth of the storm, Lord,
Calm my trembling heart.
As the waters rise about me,
Give me Your peace.
I claim Your promise of eternity
With You
Even as loneliness stalks my mind.
Through the gale, through the waves,
Help me to stand strong.
Shine the light of Your love
Across the sea of despair.
Illuminate me, please.
Be with me, Lord,
As I weather the storms of life.
May Your light ignite a flame in me
So I can shine for You.
Help me to be a beacon for You
To others also facing the storm.
Amen.

God's Jewels

Some ancient astronomers looked at the
    heavens
And saw mystical creatures.
More modern ones look and see scientific
    theories
Shaping, forming, moving the universe.
I look at the heavens and see God's
    handiwork.
Stars sparkling against the ebony velvet of
    the sky
Like laughter sparkling in the eyes of a
    child.
Strewn beyond human vision,
Galaxies woven of starlight and miracle fill
    my heart.
When I see the stars shining on high in
    silent majesty
Against the vastness of space,
I realize how very small I am in the scheme
    of things.
And yet, He loves me!
His love for me outshines the brightest of
    stars.
I am a part of His creation, a star in His
    firmament,
One of the jewels in His beautiful treasury,
A treasured child of the King!

God Don't Want Me

"God don't want me," he said and hung his head, dark hair hiding his sorrow-filled face. "You'd just be wasting your breath to pray for me."

"That's not true," she responded. "He wants all his children to come home to Him. Try Him, you'll see." She reached out to touch his shoulder, and felt him shudder through the dirty, torn t-shirt he wore.

"You don't know what I've done," he whispered. "You don't know the terrible things in my past. Laws I've broken, people I've hurt, sins I've committed. Why would God want anything to do with the likes of me?"

"He doesn't want the old behaviors. He doesn't want a list of your past actions. He wants you. He wants to give you a future. He wants your heart. He wants you, imperfections and all. He sent His Son to redeem you. He loves you."

(continued)

"Why should He love *me*? I'm a mess."

"God is the number one authority on cleaning up messes," she said, smiling. "Look in the Bible and you'll see. He cleaned up David and Rahab. He straightened out Jonah and many more. He's still pulling people out of the muck and putting them on solid ground. He can help you, too."

He lifted his head, dark eyes brimming with tears. "How do I start?"

Jesus to Salvation – a diamante

Jesus

Sinless, perfect

Praying, dying, bleeding,

Sacrificial, Innocent, Holy, Resurrected!

Cleansing, renewing, redeeming,

Offered, Gifted

Salvation

An Open Hand

Grant me, oh Lord, an open hand.
When You send gifts that You have planned
To bless me, let me grateful be
And lift my hand in praise to Thee.

An open hand that stretches e'er
To offer comfort, seeks to share
With others who, in want or need,
Will see Your love shine through my deed.

A hand of friendship in Your Name
May be the spark that lights the flame
To light their path to brighter days.
For, Lord, Your love does so amaze!

Open to help, open to give,
Lord, may I ever open live.
Open to You, open to yours.
Use me, dear Lord, to open doors.

Grant me, oh Lord, an open hand,
A heart open to Your command,
That Your love flows from You through me
And by Your Son, sets all men free.

Evening Lights

Summer evening, softly dark and warm.
Fireflies in green-gold dance flicker against
    the black velvet.
Just beyond my fingertips they loop and
    soar,
Calling to each other with their lights.
Joy expressed in dots and dashes - a secret
    code I cannot break.
Reminders of God's goodness in their play.

Far in the distance of summer's darkness,
    made small by light-years
Glisten stars against the cosmos. A grand
    display of hues
Is strewn across the palette of heaven for my
    gaze.
Flickering there in graceful orbiting dance.
Far out of reach, but not beyond my
    dreams.
Reminders of God's grandeur as they glow in
    the night.

The lights of evening seem to write
A message across my heart -
"I'm here, I love you, you are Mine.
Signed, God"

Worry War

I feel the crippling pull of fear,
The vortex swirls to suck me down.
No help I see from those nearby.
No lifeline to my desperate hands is thrown.

Yet from the dark surrounding my soul
A beam of peace shines clear and bright.
God's love dispels the hateful darkness
And fills my heart with glad new life.

The Enemy has lost the war!
A sanctuary safely hides
Me in the Father's care.
A wave of grace my soul now rides.

I cannot stop the world of change
Nor thwart the Enemy by myself.
But I can shelter find with Christ
From worry and fear. Such peace is wealth!

This Day

"This is the day the Lord has made. I will rejoice and be glad in it."
(A Golden Shovel based on Psalm 118:24, King James Version)

Did I get out of bed for this?
My blankets were warm, but the room
    is
Cold. My dreams were pleasant but
    the
Weather forecast predicts a wet day.
Now, what should I wear to go out
    into the
World? Dress up or dress down? Lord,
Give me a hint as to what the day has
In store. There are plans to be made,
Errands to run, tasks to perform. I
Can't accomplish them in my own
    will.
I want, at the end of the day, to
    rejoice
In what You have done for me and
Through me. I want this day to be
A testament to others of Your faithful
    care. I'm so glad
To know You see the day ahead in
Every detail. You know the road and
    with me, You travel it.

Inspired by a Verse

"For, lo, the winter is past, the rain is over and gone;
The flowers appear on the earth; the time of the
singing of birds is come, and the voice of the turtle is
heard in our land;"
(Song of Solomon 2:11-12, King James Version)

When long, dark days would wear me down
And all the earth seems dead and brown,
Your Word reminds me spring will come.
The birds will sing and bees will hum.

As sunshine hides away from me
And no leaves linger on the tree,
Winter has crept into my soul.
But here in Your Word, I am told

The sun will shine upon my face
And earth will be a warmer place.
The joyous flowers will burst through
And point the glory all to You.

I thank You for the promised spring
And all the treasures it will bring.
May I, in winter, ne'er lose sight
Of Your great goodness and Your light.

Once upon a Time Inside My Heart

Once upon a time, I wandered all alone.
Pain and heartache filled my every day.
Until I gave to Jesus a small corner of my
    heart
And everything then turned a different way.

Now I no longer walk alone
And days are filled with joy.
My heart is filled with God's own love
Through Mary's Baby Boy.

And once upon a time has transformed
To eternity with My sweet Lord.
He opened Heaven's gates to me
Because I opened up to His true Word.

Once upon a time, the world was sad and
    dark.
Once upon a time all hope seemed gone.
But once upon a time God sent His love to
    us
The greatest Christmas gift, His precious
    Son.

He promised through the prophets he would
    make a way
For Man to be restored within His will.
And in a quiet stable Mary birthed the
    Child.
He came to save us all. He saves us still.

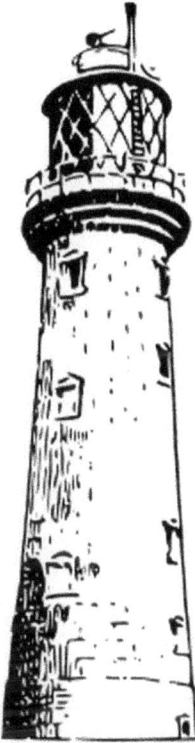

Tending
the Light of
Family

Family can take many forms. Some you are born with, some you give birth to, some you gain by marriage and some you adopt because in your heart you know you are kindred. This is for all my family members, whatever form our relationships take.

When We Danced

With you, my son, life has been a dance.
Since you started walking, any chance
To twirl, to jump, or to pirouette
Was taken with gusto. I would bet
You've covered more miles than a long-
    distance runner.

Together we've danced at sunset, dawn,
Midday and midafternoon and on.
Chased fireflies flitting through dark night
Sky. Waltzed uphill, jived downhill in flight,
Through autumn and winter, springtime
    and summer.

The last time we danced, your wedding day,
I felt as though I gave you away
Along with my right to share the dance.
Your new partner now deserves the chance
To dance with you through lives filled with
    wonder.

May life bring you music through every day.
I wish you the best in every way.
Continue your dance through years filled
with joy.
My dear dancing son, once my small
dancing boy,
I love you with all my heart, to the stars and
yonder.

Angel's Teardrops

She called them angel's teardrops,
Globs of iridescent glass in the vase.
They shimmered in the sunlight on the sill
And held the flower stems fast in place.
When someone faced a sadness or loss
She'd share one of them, saying
"Angels cry with you in your pain."
And to remind them she would be praying.
But now my mother is gone.
The angels may be weeping, too.
But she cannot give me a teardrop.
My pain is still too raw, too new.

Granddaddy's Picture

Who were you – that grim looking man in
    the photo?
The man my grandmother loved, certainly.
The father of my father, brother of my great-
    aunts and uncles.
A brakeman on the Illinois Central
    Railroad...

You were a Mason, a country boy gone to
    town.
Stern and unsmiling, I see you there in
    ancient black-and-white.
A moment printed for the future to behold,
All that I have to touch of you.

I know the facts, the dusty details, the
    stories retold.
The dates, the obituary on yellowed
    newsprint.
I know Granddaddy's picture, reprinted on
    my heart.
Oh, how I wish I could have known the man!

The Godbrother

The christening was a hurried affair --
My fault, I'm afraid.
Impending surgery would take me out of
    commission
For weeks, perhaps months.
The baby's service shouldn't wait that long.
But the priest at one parish church was
    adamant.
Christenings took place on a certain Sunday
    of the month,
Couldn't be moved.
There are rules, you know.
The door was closed.

But another clergyman was less hidebound,
    more human.
The kindly priest understood our concern
    for the child's soul
And the parents' wishes
And the medical necessities.
He arranged for us to gather
On that Friday evening:
The priest, my sister, her husband, their
    new baby,
The prospective godfather,
My mother, my five-year-old son and me.

(continued)

Our footsteps echoed in the otherwise empty
    sanctuary
As we approached the altar,
Adding a level of gravitas no choir or organ
    could have brought.
Seating my son on the first pew, I
    admonished him to stay put
And took my place at the font as the
    prospective godmother.
My son knew about church behavior,
But he had never seen a service like this
    one,
With no choir, no organ, no congregation.
Curiosity got the best of him.
Inching toward the edge of the pew,
He extended one foot, then the other and
    started to slide toward the floor.
My hissed warning did nothing to dissuade
    him.
He crept to my side.
"I'm so sorry, Father," I whispered and
    turned to herd him back to the pew.
The priest touched my arm and shook his
    head.
"Allow me," he said.
Kneeling at my son's side, looking deep into
    his eyes, he spoke.
"Do you know where you are, young man?"

(continued)

My son nodded, all serious attention.

"In a church."

"Do you know why you're here?"

"My mama's gonna be a godmother for my cousin."

"That's right. A godmother is very important."

"She's gonna teach him 'bout Jesus!"

"You're right. You love your cousin very much, don't you?"

"Oh, yes."

"Would you like to be his godbrother?"

I watched joy spread across my son's face.

He nodded agreement so vigorously I feared for his neck.

"Then come and stand here beside me," said the priest.

"I'll tell you when it's your part, okay?"

The priest stood and resumed the solemn ceremony,

Now infused with a new sort of inclusive joy.

I watched as my boy stood in quiet attention,

Eyes glued to Father's face.

When the time came, Father turned to the enthusiastic boy

And placed a hand on his shoulder.

"Will you promise to help him learn about how God loves him,

(continued)

And be his brother in Christ throughout his
    life?"
With five-year-old solemnity, my son
    nodded.
"*Yes, sir.*"
"I pronounce you his godbrother, young
    man."
Once the service was completed, we left the
    church,
A newborn and his god-family,
United by a compassionate priest who
    understood
First-time parents, newborn babies,
And a little boy who loves his cousin.

Precious in Purple

(Inspired by a photograph of my granddaughter)

She's precious in purple,
Completely happy to swirl and twirl
And dance and hug her troll.
Or smile for a photo for Grandma,
Or run to give a hug and a kiss.
Perfect fun is precious in purple.

My Son

I see you there -
Clothed in innocence,
Wrapped in dreams,
The peace of sleep upon your wearied body -
And I reflect on the day.
The tattered newspaper, not yet read,
The spilled juice,
Bread landing peanut butter side down
On the newly waxed floor.
An unexpected hug,
A small, wilted flower from some neighbor's
garden
Accompanied by an "I love you, Mommy."
I wonder at the substance of you,
Lying so peacefully.
My personal devil,
My own private angel,
My blessing -
My son.

The Touch of Daddy's Hand

It's been too long, Daddy,
For nearly two-thirds of my life
I haven't felt the touch of your hand.
When you died, my hero died,
The man who taught me to walk,
To run, to ride a bicycle, to dream.
The man I ran to when I hurt.
The man who cheered me on when I earned
    it,
Called me down when I deserved it,
But always loved me, no matter what.
The strange thing is,
Although I can't feel your hand holding
    mine,
I still feel your touch.
I feel the love you gave me in my heart.
I hear the lessons you taught me in my
    mind.
I live the faith you instilled in my soul.
I no longer feel your hand
But your gifts still touch me.
Thank you, Daddy.

Seeking Infinity

"What color is infinity?" she asked, eyes
    wide.
"Let's go on an adventure," I said. "You
    decide."
And so, we started out, my granddaughter
    and me,
To locate the answer, for her serenity.
The radiance of her smile so warmed my old
    heart
That bliss filled my whole body, every last
    part.
I couldn't help but surrender and tag along
On her quest for the color of something so
    strong
I couldn't define it. For how do you translate
A celestial concept so she could relate?
We saw velvet night skies stretched far as
    we could view,
And we tried to count droplets of cool
    morning dew.
Waves on an ocean, snow caps on a
    mountain top,
Green jungle myst'ries and shakes at a soda
    shop.

(continued)

We perused everything we two could visit.
We laughed and sang. But we found no
 clear bit of it.
My heart, melancholy, asked if I could ever
Complete this odd task or would my failure
 sever
The bond of dear love shared with this
 grandchild so sweet?
At last we sat down, took a break, shared a
 treat.
"Are we ready to try the next stage?" I asked
 then.
She looked up and smiled, a big, fat, happy
 grin.
"We've looked all up and down, and I think
 now I know.
Infinity looks just like the love grandma
 shows."
She threw her arms round me, a hug warm
 and tight.
Yes, my love for her is infinite. She's quite
 right.

Mothers Shouldn't Die in April

Mothers shouldn't die in April.
It shouldn't be allowed in the grand scheme
    of things.
After all, April is the month before May
And mothers shouldn't leave
Right before Mother's Day.
It isn't fair to taint the day of celebrating
    motherhood
In such a heartbreaking manner.
And they shouldn't die in May for the same
    reason.
It's too painful to watch others, jubilant, all
    around you
While your heart is breaking, aching, taking
Up every breath with a flood of pain.
June and July are too soon after the day
And would cast a shadow back upon it.
They should be filled with picnics and
    sunshine,
Not grieving and weeping.
August is too hot for mourning garb.
September needs mothers to get kids in
    school.
Death in October is scary already,
No need to make it scarier than usual.
November should be filled with celebrating
    thanks,
Not mourning final farewells.
December calls for joy, not pain and loss.

(continued)

Mothers shouldn't die in January.
Things should be starting fresh, not ending.
How can February celebrate love without
The love of mother? It can't be right.
And cold, cruel March would crueler still
If it were reserved for mothers dying.
There is no month appropriate for
The rending pain of a mother's death.
There is no time of year suitable for
Stopping the heart which gave you life.
Selfishly, we do not want to let them go at
    all.
If we admit the truth, we never do.
We carry them forever in our hearts.

Sisters

Sharing memories
Is the first link in the chain.
Summer's play and family outings,
Talks until all hours in the dark.
Even when we argue, we love each other.
Reading each others' faces as easily as
    books.
Sisters are joined by more than family
    name.

Sister-in-Love

(For Marilyn)

She became my dear friend by an odd sort of
 path.
Her daughter and my son are wed,
And so we became family.
Terminology for her role does not exist, that
 I know of.
Do I call her my son's mother-in-law?
Or my daughter-in-law's mother?
She is so much more than those tongue-
 twisting titles.
Not my sister by blood, but more than a
 friend,
I call her my sister-in-love.
The love of our children introduced us.
The love in our hearts connected us as
 sisters.

A Parent's Wish

Look to the heavens, little one.
See the stars twinkling above?
Each of them carries my wishes for you
And they shine with my unending love.
Choose a star, my child, for your own.
Make a wish on it as you dream.
May fulfillment be carried toward you
On the path of its silver beam.
Reach for a star, my dearest heart.
Do not limit your potential.
Stretch for the heavens from the start.
Dare to make imagined things real.
Grow in love and joy, my sweet child.
Be strong, be courageous and wise.
Let kindness guide your actions
And truth dispel the world's lies.
And the truth is waiting there in the stars.
You were made for amazing things!
God creates all children as special gifts.
Your presence such happiness brings!
So, reach for the stars and all they contain.
They are yours, and there is no doubt
You came from heaven to bless our hearts.
Possibilities are what you're about.

Generations

My Granny taught me how to bake
Hands-on at her kitchen table.
I teach my granddaughter on Alexa,
The best that I am able.

I learned to sew at Granny's knee
On a treadle sewing machine.
My granddaughter learns by watching me
Upon a computer screen.

I read to Granny from a book
The library loaned to me.
My granddaughter reads across the miles
From the device held on her knee.

Knowledge must be passed along,
From one generation to the next.
The stories and the skills we share
Give our lives their context.

As generations come along
The tools may change their parts.
The one thing that will never change?
The love between their hearts.

3rd Place, Grands Award,
Mississippi Poetry Society 2022

Water Fight

(Inspired by a drawing my granddaughter drew for
me.)

She threw.
I ducked.
The bright purple balloon
Hit the wall behind me
And disintegrated in a
Wet explosion of rubber and water.
My back is soaked —
Collateral damage from the miss.
But the cool splash feels good,
Refreshing on this hot day.

She grabs two more
And tosses them
In rapid-fire succession.
Direct hits.
My sodden clothes weigh me down
As I try to reach my own supply
Of deep blue balloons,
But she is too fast for me.
Three more hits,
Splat, splat, sploosh.

"Five hits, Gramma, I win,"
She crows, fist pumping.
As she twirls in water balloon victory,
I grab a water bomb and
Throw toward her.

(continued)

The blue bundle bursts
Against her leg,
Surprising her.
Shock fills her face.
"Gramma, you cheated!"

I shake my head.
"Tag! You're it!"
She laughs at me
And heads to her stockpile.
Game on!

The Hole

A heart-shaped hole
At the center of my universe
Draws me in
As powerfully as a tidal bore,
As inexorably as a super-giant black hole.
I circle the edges,
Drawing nearer with each orbit,
Pulled ever closer.
The darkness there calls me.
The emptiness is not there,
But here, in my arms
Where you were meant to be.
In the darkness, will I find you?
In the darkness, will my emptiness be filled?
My precious child,
You left a void which can never be filled.
You left a longing which can never be
    quenched.
Losing you changed the landscape of my life
    forever.
I ache with the torture of your absence, but
Oh, I would not have missed loving you for
    anything in the world.

Plans

My best laid plans, so carefully made,
Fall down in harsh reality's face.
Intentions cannot overcome
The anchor-drag of commonplace.

The daily jobs demand my thoughts
And fill my time with minor tasks.
The calendar and clock run on,
No care for boons my poor heart asks.

Then death, which overrules all time,
Steps in and takes a loved one's hand.
In shambles lie those well-intentioned
Thoughts of acts I might have planned.

"I should have" and "I wish I had"
Accuse me of my fallen schemes.
To say "I love you" one more time
Would be an answer to my dreams.

I laid my plans but failed to act.
The things I meant to do, undone
Until too late. Now grief wells up,
And sadness blocks the brightest sun.

Farewell, dear one. Forgive me, please.
I loved you and I always will.
Until the day we meet again,
Within my heart I hold you, still.

(First appeared in *The Tunica Voice* newspaper, 2023)

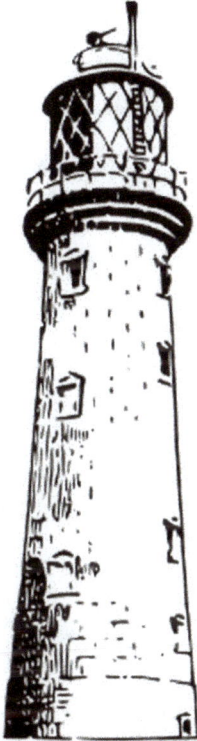

Tending the Light of Community

Our communities stretch from the folks next door to the folks across the sea. As we work to build community, we work to build a better world for ourselves and our descendants. What a precious opportunity for us to shine!

Giving Thanks

I went to a conference some years ago,
And heard of a poetry contest, so
I entered a poem or two, a seed.
No idea of where this action might lead.
The call came later -- a poetry book
Was waiting for me. My hands gently shook
To think my work appeared on its pages,
Though I'd been writing poems for ages.
So, I drove to meet Patty and claim it.
We visited in her home for a bit.
She told me what MPS meant to her.
In my heart, her words created a stir.
I joined the South Branch and found good
    friends
Who nurture me, challenge me, without end!
Then statewide, I learned, there's more of
    the same.
We've met through the channel of MPS
    name
But grown into more than poets who meet.
I've found such grand friends, so kindly and
    sweet.
Thanks for the people and poetry fine.
Thanks for the form and the rhythm and
    line.
I give thanks to God for the gift sublime
Of poetry friends and their blessed rhyme.

Dreams

Perhaps you're feeling a bit tired today.
Have aches and pains taken your joy away?
Do you mark your time on the way to the
  grave?

If you try, you'll see you're never too old
To seek a new dream or set a new goal.
Build a plan toward something new. You'll
  save

The day. Dare to dream and hark to hope.
Act like a winner to o'ercome the mope.
Accept the permission to soar which you
  gave.

Defy the lie which bids you not try,
Never to set your sights on the sky.
The lie comes from Satan, a sinful knave.

God made you for great things. Live up to
  His gift.
Let His light shine through you; you will
  others uplift.
Through His love, you will triumph. Dream
  brave!

Respondez s'il vous plait

You painted a beautiful picture,
Vibrant, colorful,
Full of depth and passion.
Your sculpture sings with elegant lines
And thought-provoking imagery.
Your work demands a response,
Even though you are long dead
Or thousands of miles away.
And so I share my feelings.
Thank you for stirring my soul
With your interpretation
Of the world around you.
Thank you for sharing the beauty you see
With the rest of us.
Thank you for daring to share your heart.

Your music grabs my feet
And starts them tapping in joy.
The lyrics lap at my mind
Like waves kissing the shore,
Leaving their high water mark
On my heart.
I hum through the day,
Dance along when I dare,
Hit "replay" time and again.
The melody sends my soul skyward,
Borne on your well crafted notes,
And soul-stirring tempos.
I had to say "thank you"
For the happiness you've given me.

(continued)

I stumbled on your writing
Quite by accident,
But such a fortunate accident!
The words you chose,
The pattern you wove with them,
The images you elicited,
Were something brand new to me.
You offered me a new perspective,
A fresh outlook.
My heart is full,
Flooded with feelings and emotions
I didn't know I could feel.
You shared knowledge
I didn't know I needed.
Because you shared your words,
I glimpsed another world.
I can never go back to who I was
Before I visited it.
Thank you for opening my eyes,
Tickling my mind, touching my life.
Thank you for your writing.

For all the creative people
In all of the creative genres,
I thank you for your contributions.
I respond to your work with
My heart and soul.
You have touched me
In ways beyond what I can count.

(continued)

It pleases me to take this time
To let you get a glimpse
Of what you have meant to me.
Perhaps my words will be as meaningful a
     gift to you
As your work has been to me.
Thank you.

A Thimble Full

A thimbleful of grief can break a heart.
A thimbleful of scorn can destroy a spirit.
A thimbleful of envy can wreck a friendship.
A thimbleful of violence can ruin a life.
A thimbleful of hate can ignite a war.

But...

A thimbleful of kindness can warm a frosty
     heart.
A thimbleful of gentleness can soothe a
     tortured mind.
A thimbleful of courage can take on a new
     challenge.
A thimbleful of love can overcome evil.
A thimbleful of faith can save a soul.
May your thimble be filled with God's
     blessings of life.

Burning Bridges

We burn bridges so easily –
With an unkind word,
A sharp retort,
A thoughtless action.
The supports collapse, and we part in
    enmity.
Mending bridges takes work.
We must repair them with kindness,
Forgiveness,
Thoughtfulness.
The bridges connect our hearts, our souls,
Until we burn them in anger.
Each time we must decide
"Is it worth the rebuilding?"
If we answer "Yes," we begin the familiar
    reconstruction process.
As I stand gazing out at the detritus of our
    latest burned connection,
The debris of our own making,
I wonder "Will it happen again? Will we
    build
Only to destroy?"
And I question whether, having been here
    before,
Will we find ourselves here again or will we
    finally
Learn the lessons needed to avoid the
    tragedy
Of burning bridges?

The Copy

"Do something wonderful, people may imitate it."
Albert Schweitzer

We all learn by studying and copying what
    came before.
To learn to speak, we copy sounds.
To learn to create words, we trace letters.
To learn to draw, we copy great artists.
To learn to write poetry, we copy great poets.
To learn to write prose, we copy great
    authors.
To learn to cook, we copy great chefs.
We don't copy to pretend it is our work,
But to learn the techniques of success,
The tools of improvement.

Why can't we do the same with life.
To learn to live kindly, we can study and
    copy altruistic people.
To learn to live generously, we can copy
    philanthropists.
To learn to live peacefully, we can copy
    peacemakers.
To learn to live wisely, we can copy people of
    wisdom.
If we copy the attributes we want to perfect,
We can become better people.
If we become better people,
We can make the world a better place.

Fury

The storm attacks in mindless rage
As sky conditions set the stage
For wind and rain and surging tide
To strike the coastal countryside.
The weary people batten down.
Fury strikes each city and town.

Wildfire scorches as it rolls
Across terrain. It takes its tolls
In structures, plants and memories.
Behind its line, denuded trees
And smoldering ruins fill the land.
It sweeps away the signs of man.

Anger destroys as it lashes
Out. It crushes and it smashes
Everything, leaving only pain.
Love may not come to bloom again
In hearts once seared bare by blind rage.
Anger locks the heart in a cage.

Fury comes in many dark ways.
Behavior or nature, it plays
Out in devastation and pain.
We build, rebuild to fall again.
Wherever fury rears its head
Spread love and peace and hope instead.

Collateral Damage

You are angry.
You seethe and boil with rage.
Your thoughts are consumed
With hate
And revenge,
Payback for the injury or slight
You feel someone dealt to you.
And in your blind anger, you lash out.
You strike at anyone,
Anyone who may be even close to your
     target.
You don't think about who else you hurt
Besides your desired victim.
In the real world, that's known as
Collateral damage,
Innocents caught in the vicious crossfire
Of ill-considered or uncaring actions.
Is that what you want?
Do you want to hurt people,
People you may not even know,
People who have done you no harm?
People who may care about you,
Maybe even love you?
In that case, congratulations.
You have succeeded spectacularly.
I hope you and your hate will be very happy
     together.
But beware.

(continued)

Take warning.
Your actions create debts which must be
    paid.
If not in this world, then in the next,
The bill *will* come due.
Your very soul may be
Collateral damage in the end.

The Most Important Songs

"What's your favorite song?" she asked.
"Mine is..." and she named a recent hit
Released by a current pop icon.
I was hard pressed to respond to the young
    lady.
My knowledge of current music is,
(Shall I admit it?) rather lacking.
And there are too many tunes residing
In the audio library of my mind to pick only
    one.
"I can't name just one favorite," I said,
"But let me tell you about two songs
Which have been very important in my life."
She nodded assent, puzzlement filling her
    eyes.
"The first is 'Jesus loves the little children.'
When I sing the song, I am reminded
That every one of us,
Every child
Of every color
In every land is His precious child.
We are family, beloved by Him.
The second is 'Jesus loves me,'" I said
"Because it taught me of His love for all,
Including me.
When I feel alone,
Or discouraged
Or weak,

(continued)

I remember His love,
His encouragement,
His strength.
I can go on, because He loves me.
I suppose I could consider those my favorite
    songs.
Certainly, they are the most important ones
    in my life."
I looked at her, expecting ridicule.
She smiled and leaned toward me to
    whisper,
"I love them, too."

Your Story

God writes your story, day by day.

Each scene, each paragraph, each line.

For latest edits, pause and pray.

Your life plays out in His design.

Common Ground

If I reached out in friendship to you,
Could we meet on some common ground?
Or would old enmities keep us apart?
Would ancient hurts bring our best efforts
    down?

Generational scars we both bear.
Can we use them as common ground?
Let's rise above the wrongs of the past,
Lest ancient hurts bring our best efforts
    down.

Looking back at the lessons we've learned
We can meet on that common ground.
Yet brandishing them as clubs o'er our
    heads
Lets ancient hurts bring our best efforts
    down.

We cannot mankind's history undo.
Wrong was done, and by that we're bound.
If we go forward sworn to do right,
Then ancient hurts cannot bring us down.

So, I reach out in friendship to you,
Offer peace as our common ground.
May we, as brethren, walk forward as one,
And ancient hurts be buried and down.

Planting the Tree

Ms. Parks, did you aim to be a gardener,
To assist at the seeding of a movement?
Did your heart pound fast with pride or with
    fear,
Or maybe both,
When you held your seat on that bus and
    nurtured the seed?
Thank you for your courage to act.

Little Addie Mae Collins, Denise McNair,
Carole Robertson, and Cynthia Wesley,
Did you know your short lives would count
    for so much?
Cut down by hate before your time,
Your blood fertilized the soil of the cause of
    justice
And educated the world
As the horrors of segregationists became
    apparent.
We thank you for your innocence,
Even as we mourn your martyrdom.

Rev. Shuttlesworth, as you looked at the
    rubble
Of what had been God's house
Before hateful men set their bomb,
Did you see the hearts which would be
    touched
And eyes which would be opened by this
    event?

Thank you for your stewardship,
For giving justice a place to bloom, pushing
    up through the ashes.

Dr. King, when you had that dream and
Climbed to that mountaintop,
Did you visualize how long the journey
    would take
For the rest of the world?
Did you understand how abysmally slowly
    we would come along?
Thank you for marking the trail for us with
    your very lifeblood.

Alabama provided a garden to nurture the
    tree called Freedom.
The seedling was cultivated and bloomed in
    Montgomery,
In Birmingham, in Selma and many more
    communities.
Carried on buses, and the backs of peaceful
    marchers,
And in the planes of the Tuskegee Airmen,
The sapling made its way across Alabama,
Across the South and then the nation,
A tree of freedom growing each day.
Watered by the blood of martyrs
And the sweat of marchers
And the faith of those who knew
God created us all and created us all
    human,

(continued)

That tree still grows,
Still reaches for maturity,
Still strives to achieve the day when all
  God's children,
Every hue and color,
Can stand together in peace and love
In the shade of that beautiful tree in God's
garden, planted in Alabama.

First Place, Alabama Poetry Society
Fall 2024 Contest, BKC Award

Shaking It Off

In spite of Taylor Swift's best advice,
I find I cannot shake it off.
My shaker is empty.
The critics and commentators
Send arrows of negativity at me.
They sting, they stick, they hurt.
The world throws so much turmoil,
Human suffering, upheaval, disruption
Until I can't shake off the pain.
Perhaps if the world could shake off hate,
And greed and lust and envy,
If evil would shake off its control
Of human hearts and souls,
I might be able to shake off the fear,
The pain, the hurt I experience when
I survey the human condition.
But I can't just shake off the grief I feel
When I see hungry children, displaced
    families,
Homes destroyed and crops leveled.
I can't shake the feeling of sadness
Which grips my heart at each new death,
Each assault on humanity.
I can't shake it off.
Can you?

In the Waiting Room

The chairs are carefully designed to be
    sanitized with ease,
Not to be comfortable for long periods.
The soothing background music wends
    softly through the room,
Just an undertone really.
Meant to calm and encourage rather than
    entertain.
Tight groups of people, scattered in various
    corners,
Hold hands or weep or whisper on cell
    phones.
They enter or leave by turns,
Seeking information
Or coffee or other needs.
Medical staff come and go, approaching
    families they recognize,
Asking by name for those they don't.
Update delivered, they disappear again,
Back through the forbidden doors.
Lord, as we wait here,
Trusting a loved one to human skills,
Help us to remember
You are the One in charge.
The Great Physician,
The Ultimate Healer.
We pray You will order their minds,
Guide their hands, calm their hearts.

(continued)

As we sit in this earthly waiting room,
We sit also at Your throne
As we turn our hearts toward You in prayer,
Resting in Your promise of eternal life.

'Til Then

There are those that I have loved, whose
    company I have known.
And some of them have gone ahead to wear
    a heavenly crown.

To them I make this promise: I know we'll
    meet again,
And so, I'll keep your memory close and
    treasure it — 'til then.

And when we greet each other beyond sweet
    Heaven's door
I'll trade the memory for the fact. Until then,
    I'll endure.

Some lives I'm privileged still to share as
    family and friends.
You lift me up when I get down no matter
    what life sends.

(continued)

We go through things together. On each
    other we depend.
I know, though, that someday we'll part. I'll
    treasure you, 'til then.

And comfort take in knowing that though we
    part awhile,
Eternity is ours to share. 'Til then, I'll wait
    and smile.

When my turn comes to say "farewell," I
    hope that you can say
That life was better for us both because we
    shared the way.

And forward looking, glimpse the day we'll
    meet and laugh again.
Remember me with happiness and
    joyousness 'til then.

Know too that when we meet there Eternity
    we'll spend
With Him who gave His life for us. Live
    faithfully 'til then.

Love and Death

Love doesn't end with death.
It just stretches a little farther
And reaches from here to Heaven.
Love doesn't die with the loved one.
The seed has been planted
And the flower of love waits
For the right moment
To burst into bloom again
In Heaven's garden.
Love renews itself,
Like a butterfly emerging from a cocoon.
Love doesn't stop with the last heartbeat.
The rhythm of the dance simply changes.
Love, once truly found,
Cannot be lost,
Only out of sight for a time.
Love provides the compass
To show the road back to each other
In God's time.

The Silence

"In the end, we will remember not the words of our
enemies, but the silence of our friends"
                    - Martin Luther King Jr.

The verdict is in.
I have been found guilty
By reason of inaction.

When you needed me most,
When you needed the heat of
Passionate support,
I offered only lukewarm affirmation.

At a time when one more soul
Standing firm against oppression
Might have made a difference,
I wavered on the front line.

I found somewhere else I had to be,
Something else I had to do.
I failed you through my absence,
Through my silence,
Through my inconstancy.

Can you ever forgive me?
Will you let me stand by you now,
Joining the battle against hate,
Against bigotry?

I cannot undo my past failings.
I can only go forward.

Controlled Burn

Tree people call it a controlled or prescribed
        burn,
Lighting the forest floor or dry prairie,
To burn off the undergrowth and deadfall.
When conditions are right for best control,
They start the flame.
Fire clears away useless detritus
And allows fresh, new growth,
Healthy growth.
It reduces the chance of devastating
Uncontrolled conflagrations later
In the case of an errant lightning strike
Or carelessly flung spark.
The ash created helps to feed the surviving
        flora.
Proactive care for the ecosystem.

Maybe we need a controlled burn in life.
A tidy, organized way to remove
Dead relationships and deadly habits
Which hold us back.
If we get rid of the people and things
Choking us,
Hindering us,
Entangling us,
Cluttering the soil around our roots,
We can grow taller.
We can live stronger.

(continued)

We can thrive
Outside of the negative shadow they cast.
We reduce the chance of
A devastating emotional firestorm
In the wake of a hurtful event.
Controlled disconnection, prescribed
shedding
Of unproductive relationships
Can give us better conditions to thrive;
To bloom, to be the best we can be.
Perhaps the time has come to prescribe
A cleansing fire.

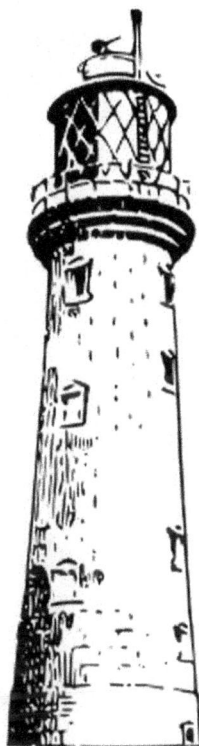

Tending
the Light of
Writing

What drives a writer? The words nag you
until you let them out as a poem, a story,
an essay. The more you write, the better
you get, so tend the light of your creativity!

So, You Think You Want To Be a Poet

I looked at myself in the mirror and asked
    the question
Which was weighing like a mountain on my
    soul.
Against its crushing tonnage, I struggled to
    find the answer.
At last, I dared to ask it out loud.

So, you think you want to be a poet,
Think you can be a poet?
Whatever gave you such an idea?
Yes, I'm sure you love and appreciate
The clever phrasings of William
    Shakespeare,
The drama of Nikki Giovanni,
The tragedy of Emily Dickinson,
The romance of Elizabeth Barrett Browning,
The courage of Maya Angelou, and more.
That's a starting point, certainly.
But the end of the journey? Never.
You may be able to rattle off definitions of
Iambic pentameter,
Blank verse,
Rondeaus and villanelles,
Couplets and triplets and quatrains,
Forms and formats
And poetic devices.
But will knowing them make you a poet?
Think again!

All those dozens of homophones
At your fingertips?
Useless!
It takes much more than just rhyming
    words
If you want to be a poet.
Here are a few tips.
Forget everything you think you know
About language and rhyme schemes
And proper pronunciation.
Unlearn the image of idyllic words
Spilling from your pen in a flood
Of elegant language.
Open your heart instead of your head.
Knowledge helps, but it isn't enough.
Techniques are handy, but only as starting
    points.
It takes hard work to be a poet!
Those lines don't get written just in ink.
They form from sweat dripping down
Your face as you wrestle with worrisome
    words.
They take shape from blood you've spilled
From veins you've opened fighting the fear
Of never, ever finding the right phrase
To finish the verse.
You'll rise and you'll dive,
Shining, fading, burning like a star,
Slamming, jamming,

(continued)

Laughing, crying, sighing, singing,
Quenched like Toledo steel,
Nurtured like an exotic orchid.
Smooth as silk, staccato as castanets,
Beautifully elegant, coarsely crude,
Tasteful, common,
Uptown, downtown, back of town,
Out of town, coming, going,
Crawling, walking, running,
Soaring, falling,
Blessing, cursing poetry.
It comes from your heart
And plays with your mind.
It grabs you by the gut
And twists and never lets go!
Whatever subject you write about,
Whatever form you write it in,
How ever many lines you choose to write,
How ever many years you continue to write,
Poetry will take over your life
If you give it a chance.
So, you think you want to be a poet?
Then have at it.
Start writing and revising,
Reading and rereading
And editing some more.
Take on the beast and begin.
May the best words win!

Editorial Comment

I watched the pages as she turned them,
And wished I could read her mind
As easily as she read the words.
Did she like what she saw?
Did my efforts please her?

No glimmer of expression crossed her face
As she worked her way
Through my hard work.
The days of writing,
More days of rewriting.

My heart, poured out in each line,
Carried a flood of hopes
And dreams and prayers
From my mind to the page,
Now to her eyes.

Would she be touched by what I'd written?
Would the phrases she saw there offend
    her?
Or would she recognize intent
And see the message tucked away
Behind the fiction I described?

She read on, eyes moving to and fro,
Otherwise a sculpture in flesh,
Part of the chair in which she sat.
My mind raced in fear,
Prepared for icy disapproval.

(continued)

At last, she raised her head.
Her tear-glazed gaze met mine,
"I didn't know," she whispered.
"You never said anything before.
Why didn't you tell me how you felt?"

The Key to the Treasure

Within a vault, built stout of stone,
A treasure waits. Wouldst call thine own?
Then listen to the secret true
Which I would freely share with you.
To open up this treasure trove,
Look deep inside. What do you love?
Identify your calling, then
Pursue its study without end.
As more you learn, richer you grow
In ways which now you can't yet know.
'Tis education holds the key
To set this precious treasure free.

Sending My Children

I send my verses out into the world,
Out of the shelter of my watchful care.
They are my children, born of my very heart,
My God-given creativity,
With a lineage tracing back to
Nursery rhymes and childhood songs.
Their pedigree includes troubadours,
Romantics, and historians.
Written in my heart's blood,
My thoughts grow on the page
One word at a time.
Phrases build to lines and lines to full
    poems,
Some rhymed, some not.
Some true, some fiction.
But always my beloved offspring.
I work with them,
Nurture them,
Love them
And, when I find the courage,
I send my verses out into the world.

The Words

Words rule my life.
Some days, the words are kind,
Encouraging me, cheering me on,
Offering hope and joy.
Other days, the words are cruel
     taskmasters,
Demanding my heart's blood
And devouring my thoughts,
Replacing them with unrhythmic syllables
And unrhymed lines.
Oh, but some days, those special days,
The words are a safe harbor,
A place where magic happens.
On those days, the words allow me
To paint with them,
Creating murals of ideas which stretch
As long as the Great Wall of China,
Higher than the stratosphere,
Deeper than the ocean's bottom,
As wide and glittering as the Milky Way.
The word pictures can touch hearts,
Reach minds,
Overcome obstacles and
Change the world.
They make me feel like a paintbrush
Held in God's hand,
Decorating the whole planet with His love.

(continued)

My words can fly, circling around the
    equator
And from Pole to Pole.
On those days, I am so honored
To be a writer, to be in God's plan
And so grateful to be connected
Through Him to the wonder of
The Words.

Poets Popping Poems

We're poets come together
In a room of tea and wonder.
We've overcome the weather,
Found luscious treats to plunder.
The words we build bring magic
To our hearts and souls and minds.
Some bright and fun, some tragic,
We heard poems of all kinds.
When poets join in rhyming
The words fly hot and fast.
And in the poems' timing
We find ideas which will last.

The Vine and the Verse

Like kudzu climbing a telephone pole,
    A verse can climb into your heart.
The words creep upon you, entwine you,
    Becoming a part of you.
They touch you in places you've forgotten
existed,
        Remind you of memories long treasured,
           Take you to new experiences.
The verse can capture you as completely
    As the verdant vine captures its pole.
When the poet strikes a chord
    Upon your heartstrings
        With words and emotions,
           Rhythms and rhymes,
They move together in sweet harmony.
You will hear a gentle melody in your soul,
    As sweet as the song of the breeze
        Singing through the kudzu vines.

Celebrate Poetry Month

If you find you like rhyme,

You'll have a great time

Hearing poetry read

Or recited instead,

As a genre we celebrate-

Come on, don't be late!

I Thought to Write a Poem

I thought to write a poem,
A perfect poem –
One to touch the hearts and minds
Of all who read it.
I planned to make it beautiful,
Steeped in lyric words,
With classic iambic pentameter rhythm
Beating like a human heart.
I pondered on which elegant form to use
And debated the rhyme scheme with
    myself.
Oh, it would be the grandest poem, I
    thought.
The very best poem I'd ever written,
Possibly the best poem in history.
It would change the world.
I mulled my ideas every day,
Made notes and starts and
Wrote down phrases to use.
As days went by, I kept on thinking,
Kept on planning,
Kept on pondering.
Then came the day when I realized
My great unwritten poem
Had missed the submission deadline.
I guess I'll have to change the world
Tomorrow.

Critique

I bring my heart and soul,
Poured out on a page
And offer them to you
For your consideration.
Can you see the dreams
And hopes and fears I share?
Or do you see just words?
Do you feel my uncertainty
Or only your own power?
Is your heart one for helping
Or hurting?
Will your critique help me grow as a writer
Or stop me from ever writing again?
You have power in your words,
Authority in your hands.
How will you wield it?
Your words can help me find my way
Or cause me to lose it forever.
You can break my heart
Or build my spirit.
Let kindness and wisdom guide you,
Remembering your own vulnerability
As you offer a critique.

The Gathering of Poets

If crows form a murder and lions join a
    pride,
What do we call poets in a crowd?
Zebras may dazzle and fishes may school,
But how to tag poets out loud?
Sheep come in a flock, mules in a pack,
Cows and horses show up in their herds.
But when poets gather, what shall we say
To ensure everyone speaks their words?
Geese in a gaggle hiss, each in turn.
Exultations of skylarks swirl 'round.
An unkindness of ravens brings gloom to
    the sky.
But poets uplift with their sound.
Sharks in their shiver bring fear to the sea.
Poets bring beauty and thought.
Words and rhythms share feelings and
    more,
Whether verses are rhymed or are not.
Poets gather in spirit with those gone before
And those in the future to come.
We offer our poems and souls on the page
And hope in your heart they find home.

Honorable Mention, The New York Poetry Forum Award, National Federation of State Poetry Societies Contest (2022)

The Process of Writing

Letters dance around my mind like a flock of
    joyous birds.
They dip and soar, swirl and swoop then
    settle down to roost as words.

The words in ragged rows align, tired and
    sagging pasture fences,
Then slowly straighten and adjust their
    ranks to make up sentences.

As sentences begin to join, the paragraphs
    each coalesce.
From the dancing letters there now comes a
    hopeful message.

Father, bless these simple words and send
    them speeding on their way
That in some needful life they would a
    Christian difference make today.

Lament

So often I feel
as though I'm on the outside
looking in on a party
I wasn't invited to.
Life often feels that way,
As though I were the
Poor hungry waif
Standing outside the bakery
With my nose pressed against the window.
I just don't fit in.
But, oh, when I write,
When the words pour out of me in a torrent,
A tidal surge which cannot be checked,
Then I'm alive and feel as though I belong.
In the embrace of the words,
I feel safe and loved.
In the flow of the words,
I feel alive and relevant.
In the words, I feel I've come home.
The words are my food and drink,
My water and air.
They are my life.

Poets Win by Writing

Poets win by writing down
The rhythmic dreams they hold.
Each verse carries thoughts profound
And challenges quite bold
So other folks might hear the call
And rise to aid the cause.
We meet in poetry's vast hall.
Our goal is not applause,
But rather, touching human hearts
And spurring kindly deeds.
We win when readers make their starts
To meet some other's needs.
One verse won't sway the whole Earth
Or rescue every life.
But each line carries its own worth.
Bring out the drum and fife!
Thus, poets lead the human charge
To make a better world.
Each poem, whether small or large,
Becomes a flag unfurled.

Let the Poetry Roll!

If, like me, you love rhyme, you'll have a
    great time
As we celebrate those who write verse.
Hearing poetry read or recited instead,
Adds gold to the mind's empty purse.

As the words roll along like a dearly loved
    song,
Let the joy fill your heart as you hear.
Good times roll with the rhymes and blank
    verses. Like chimes
And holiday bells, they bring cheer.

Brilliant images grow with each verse and
    you know
That the good times do not have to end.
Share a verse from a book or an idea you
    cook
In the cauldron of dreams. Weave and blend

Words and phrases with art you find deep in
    your heart.
You must know there is no Wrong or Right
To the feelings you bring with each line
    which you sing.
Let Good Poetry Times Roll day and night.

Previously appeared in the Creative Minds Writers
Group 2023 anthology

The Untitled Page

Blank, pristine, beckoning,
The untitled page awaits.
It holds nothing
Yet potentially holds everything.
New worlds,
New lives,
New adventures.
Blossoming loves,
Kinetic journeys,
Explosive events and
Calming scenes.
The untitled page
Offers a blank canvas
To the ink of a poet's pen,
The paint of an author's words.
It opens the door to
Infinite images,
Limitless possibilities.
Untitled, yes,
Blank, perhaps for the moment.
But empty?
Never!
Come...
The untitled page awaits.

Previously appeared in the Walt Whitman Two
Hundred and Five anthology

Let Them Go

(Inspired by the Disney musical "Frozen")

The page sits blank on my tablet tonight,
Not a sentence to be seen.
There's a character inside me --
Is she virtuous or mean?
Supporting cast develops
As the plot proceeds.
I have to write it out,
An author's what it needs.
Get in the world, go out and live,
That's the free advice non-writers give.
They think me strange to write so long,
But they're all wrong!
Let them go, let them go,
Can't hold them back from the page.
Let them go, let them go,
Words can comfort or enrage.
Words can hurt
But words can heal.
Let the words ring out...
Take an idea and make it real!
It's funny how some people
Think writing's just a lark.
Take a pen and paper
And go hang out in the park.
It's time to share the words I write,
To let my storyline take flight.

(continued)

No nom de plume to hide behind –
This is mine!
Let them go, let them go,
Can't hold them back from the page.
Let them go, let them go,
My writing is my stage.
Words can hurt
But words can heal.
Let the words ring out...
They never see the craft
Behind the things they read.
And if you cut my veins,
It's printer's ink I bleed.
My words can shape ideas,
Incense and entertain.
No way to hold them back,
They'll bubble out again!
Let them go, let them go,
Can't hold them back from the page.
Let them go, let them go,
My writing is my stage.
Words can hurt
But words can heal.
Let the words ring out!
Writers take ideas
And make them real!

Previously appeared on YouTube at
https://youtu.be/5eg-B21aPZI.

Author's Note

Thank you for sharing this journey with me. I am honored to serve as the Mississippi Poetry Society's 2025 Poet of the Year and delighted to present this collection of my poetry to you.

MPS has been a place of growth and learning for me, as well as a source of amazing friends and mentors. If you are a poet seeking a nurturing group, please check out the Mississippi Poetry Society at www.misspoetry.net.

Within the group, we share learning, publication and contest opportunities and more. Feedback on your work, times to read aloud and more are all part of MPS meetings. We share connections with other poetry societies through our membership in National Federation of State Poetry Societies.

Our meetings take place across the state. We would love to meet you at one of them.

Let your poetic light shine!

Meet Mary Beth Magee

Mary Beth draws on her curiosity and love of research to explore the world around her and write about it. A New Orleans native and true GRITS (Girls Raised in the South), she also has lived in St. Bernard Parish and south Mississippi, with stints in Chicago and northern California. Back home in Pearl River County, she is content to stay put at last.

She grew up in the Ninth Ward of New Orleans and learned the joys of beignets and French bread at an early age. And yes, she sucks 'da heads on crawfish and loves a shrimp po-boy, dressed, please!

She first saw her name in print as a juvenile book reviewer and poetry contributor for her hometown paper on the Young People's Page and hasn't stopped writing since. Over the years, her writing topics grew to cover news and feature articles, book and movie reviews, training materials, greeting cards, short fiction, poetry, and church bulletins. Her work has appeared in local and national professional publications, local newspapers and several online sites. Her first novel, *Death in the Daylilies*, and its sequel, *Ambush at the Arboretum*, are available as are many story collections and anthologies in which she appears. She is an award-winning poet, with several poetry collections to her credit.

Her website (www.LOL4.net) provides the gateway to her work. She also writes "Barnabas on the Road – the Adventures of a Traveling Zebra," a series of Christian children's stories featuring a toy zebra. Besides writing, she conducts online training classes for REALTORS™.

She is the proud mother of an adult son, who has married a lovely lady and made Mary Beth a delighted grandmother.

She holds a Bachelor of Science degree in Psychology, focusing on adult learning. It only took her 30 years to finish it! She is honored to be a member of Phi Kappa Phi, Pi Gamma Mu, and PsyChi.

As an author, she belongs to several writing groups in the southern region – in addition to Mississippi Poetry Society – and enjoys learning more about her craft from all of them. She shares her knowledge through presentations across the country.

Most important of all, she is a born again Christian who thanks God every day for her salvation and the joys of family and the written word.

Books by Mary Beth Magee

Poetry

Songs of Childhood, Echoes of Years
Life and All: The Journey
The World through Tears
Paw Prints on My Heart
Grandpa's Mustache
Tending the Light

Nonfiction

Devotions from the Road of Life
Volume 1: Hitting the Road
Volume 2: Devotions for Caregivers

The Creative Spark

Creativity: An Essential Tool for the Real
World
Jumpstart the Creativity in Your Writing
Sixty Days to Greater Writing Creativity
Storytime Crafts, Games and Gifts Using
Recycled and Inexpensive Items

Fiction

The (LOL)⁴ Mysteries
Death in the Daylilies: Volume 1
Ambush at the Arboretum: Volume 2

Fiction (continued)

The Cypress Point Chronicles
(short story anthologies)

Volume 1: Cypress Point Confidences
Volume 2: A Cypress Point Christmas
Volume 3: Cypress Point Spirit

Books for Children

Grandpa's Mustache
Pearl's Pool: Volume 1 of Pearl the Turtle
Pearl Makes a Friend: Volume 2 of Pearl
the Turtle
Some More Cows
The Promise Wreath

See more at www.LOL4.net.

Index of Verses

Index of Quotations